the INVITATIONS

Published in the UK by Beacon Books and Media Ltd
Earl Business Centre, Dowry Street, Oldham, OL8 2PF, UK.

www.beaconbooks.net

ISBN: 978-1-915025-86-9 Paperback
ISBN: 978-1-915025-87-6 Hardback
ISBN: 978-1-915025-88-3 eBook

Cataloging-in-Publication record for this book is available from the British Library

Cover design by Raees Mahmood Khan

the INVITATIONS

Lutfi Al-Nufoury

BB
BEACON BOOKS

theCONTENTS

The Acknowledgements

theACKNOWLEDGEMENTS

Thank you to my wonderful parents.
To all the helpers sent to me by The One.
To Paul Abdul Wadud Sutherland for his poetic
guidance and correspondence.
And to *The Jungle Book* for continuing to inspire me,
though it is long since Mowgli has grown up
(and Shere Khan is dead and gone).

For Lubaba

بِسْمِ اللَّهِ الرَّحْمَنِ الرَّحِيمِ

In the name of Allah,
the Most Merciful, the Most Compassionate

Prologue

welcome
she saw you smiling once
inviting in
the light within
and when you smiled again
the whole world opened
up her deep and varied vaults
to try and wrestle
you away
from what is real

The prayer

the prayer the prayer
the cradle that rocks me
is the prayer

the hand that stops me
is the prayer

my rocks are smashed
by the sea of the prayer

trees splintered
hearts open
sap running
laid bare

Mowgli

half and half boy
all the jungle knows it
half smile half naked
boy what a predicament

he loved it though
a mad world full
of wild souls
so vivid these animals

it felt like home
dark leaves ripe fruit
swirling rapids and
woozy evenings

friends with a panther
and a big brave bear
they love you
but listen

young blood
mancub
you will never fit in
and that is your mark

of true innocence

Mafi shay (nothing)

ما في شيء

mafi shay
left over when the
day closes

a thousand little fishes
slip away to leave me
in the dark water

and now a cacophony
of whispers
and then nothing

Haneda airport

I wander without knowledge
the fleeting sun is hot pink
hidden between hotels

I tilt my chin towards the light
it's toasty warm and all around
foreign signs are glowing red fruit

later whilst running past
the washing lines
at the frayed edge of the city

I peer over at
the winding road
that reaches for the airport

dark and squat it sits upon the sea
the backs of planes
glittering like jewels

Lift off

you can only do this
with perfect timing

first you neatly roll
up your shadow

and pack it away
you may need it later

then you locate yourself
that should be easy

place both hands firmly
on the mantle of your worries

and simply lift them off

Killer

a squirrel zig zagging
checked its run
and for a moment
I cared so much
I saw it try to adjust

the lorry came
at seventy miles per hour
all ugly weight and ugly power

The act of dying

to die doesn't take long
they say
let your mind slip
into hay and fresh wilds

if someone said that
to you I'd say
don't be fooled
get your stuff

and go birdwatching
if only for one
frost-bitten day
take dark chocolate

and strong coffee
you'll be steeled
by the flask
look to the open

canopy of the heavens
you know that
it cannot all be
for nothing

Parenthood (beginnings)

do not fear dreams
stay close to your mount
be strong my love
and remember your *Rabb*

Until

the feel of losing someone
the thought of eating clay
breadcrumbs becoming atoms
the thread of Islam thinning
your words upturned in pain
the faithful staying faithful
the sun will keep on rising
on this white haired world
only until

Qibla

balanced over my mihrab
there is no God but God
bound up in a skilled
calligrapher's knot

and I stared intent
on untangling those
rare black boughs
but they were endless

The desert is so wide

near a small stone mosque
old stones very old
long haired smiling goat
holds my gaze
wide green eyes
and vertical slit pupil
long haired comfortable
in yourself the warm breeze
buffeting soft walls you
lean on the air
elsewhere in this
land are bony sheep
small space demarcated by
wire pens dilapidated
restricting them like so
even though the desert
is so nice and wide
sometimes like you
I can't move
in all directions I'm held
escorted to stillness
by my own doing
enough
it is patience
I know it is time for patience

Balloo

there are ways to protect
as if you take all
the painful mess
and badness

soak it up in your broad
furry chest and then
do your best to make
the child laugh

twist the darkness
into a game to
make the child laugh
like a little lantern

get mad baby
you will be strengthened
and so the cycle
begins again

Hand in hand

nothing can undo the knots
in this internal language
no amount of ink
can get me what I need

patience comes as seldom
as the Northern Lights'
weird green ribbon
graces skies

when hand in hand
soul and nafs
put down swords
and just enjoy the view

Resolve

real resolve
in the scanning eye
of the white-tailed eagle

leaving loved ones
she banks on a
towering sea breeze
and enters true night

the map is black
all is quiet
her huge wings
beat the cold air

I hope she knows the way

Hippocratic

heart at thirty
beats per minute
needs pacing
your saturation dropped
we're racing against
time to stop your
sepsis it's a shame
that you were bed-bound
for two weeks you'll
need to drink more fluids
your kidneys won't
survive the wedding
this injection stops your
clots and that one went
to market now your
rash is drug related
and your mood is locked forever
and you asked me will
I die the answer's yes
it's definitely yes
regardless of
my long degree
and what I claim to know
you are my only patient now
I cannot leave your side
until we teach each other something

Runner

green and gold London
afternoon fading
runner sweats
carrying home
a bunch of flowers

(it's Mother's Day)

The split moon

they say that meeting
your child is like meeting
a piece of your own
flesh and blood

I concur and say
I'm still waiting for this
massive wave of love
to crest

deep in my chest
it rumbles slow and burns
her name expands
each letter like a newborn star

the Prophet ﷺ
lost six children
in his lifetime
Ruqayya Zaynab

Umm Kulthum
Qasim Abdullah
and Ibrahim
six stars died

yes Muhammad ﷺ
split the moon
but after his
six stars died

his tears dried
he gave people his time
and smiled his steady
blessed smile

like the sun's warm
smile greets the
mountain tops
every day at dawn

I'm torn
is the divided moon
more of a miracle
or his patience?

Just dinosaurs

my first love was the dinosaurs
deep beneath unopened caves
and hidden from the winds

formidable sea creatures
whose rolling eyes have lost
their sight and huge snapping

predators whose jawbones
so elegantly formed seem
too perfect just to crush and kill

perhaps their real purpose
was to die and strike a pose
in this gently lit museum

and even still on certain days
I wish to climb inside displays
to hang around with Allosaurus

Iguanodon Oviraptor and what's
his name with the long neck
just for old time's sake

I'd like to swap my house for
the Cretaceous just to taste a
time when things were

not so raw and strange
before that grand old meteor
when life was just as simple

as Tyrannosaurus Rex

The irises

like broken smoke
this world is writhing
away from us

always
we call it the *dunya*
so obviously

don't put your hope in it
please don't enlist yourself
watching the irises

bold purple gold
bursting out
to say hello

remind yourself
it's all just images
ephemeral warp

yet still what's inside
may endure beyond
and then beyond

The buffet

if left unchecked
with all these cuisines
a soul could suffocate

Drought

without you I look up
and all the stars
seem wobbly
one by one they resign
they can't do their jobs properly
anymore
this is the year
that my beard
has begun to turn grey
you are my next in line
yet even further
away
than long awaited rain

Getting out

another one
tries to twist the sky
around its struts

stainless bridges
glass grey fluency
it joins the rest

by itself vulgar mediocre
but it's hard to resist
the charm of the whole

project moody dark bricks
hot meat on charcoal
give me more flavour

we walk below
on chopped up
bits of campus

tangled bikes
clean and dirty city
quiet corners for the residents

blouses fresh suits
whereas the rest
of us come in and out

like breaths taken by
a somewhat tired
set of lungs

I miss this place
already rusting
metal pulls on

heartstrings
but so glad to
be homebound

as we merge with
the ring road like
a river flowing back

to the sea

Fat Smith

split is one way to see it
when you're born like us

Anglo Arabian horses
do very well I'm told
and so I'll hold my head
high as a stallion

of course on the outside
I'll still be polite
the flight of an Arab horse
frothing at the mouth

tearing across deserts
is enough for me
let alone my Syrian
grandmother sitting

cross legged in her
turquoise velvet dress
always calling for a kiss
I couldn't cross the room

without being caught
by her loving arms
and my English grandad
climbing back

into college after curfew
with his slacks and tweed
jacket sneaking
off to the chip shop

a handsome young
man he was
and a skilful fly half
he used to kick

but his range was short
I asked him who
did the long kicks
he told me Fat Smith

that's what we used to call him
and his face creased
up in merry laughter
he was eighty eight

but in that moment
his years were gone
he was that grammar
school boy again

his father was a glass blower
and in her teens
his mother worked
down at the mill

Pigeons

it is a well-known fact that
pigeons eat coins and air
see the living with feathers
covered in sparkling petrol
see the dead with breasts
split open as if gulping in the
city for one last time and see
that strange white pigeon
odd furry feet limping across
the busy pavement like
a veteran of some sort of
ongoing war wait a second
did that thing just smile

If I could

I'd ask the moon
to always keep your room well lit
on nights when I'm away

Shushed

look
no one wants to be shushed
but sometimes it's good for us

The limit

the old gnarled olive tree
kissed so many times
by wind that sometimes loves

and sometimes hates
the silvered limbs
that gently guard this villa

it is said that the very limit
of our understanding
was represented by a tree

branching to infinity
its roots are always deeper
how many words did that

bark absorb
how many years of silence
how many travellers

sat for a while
and remembered loved ones
under amiable sun

and how many thought
of God whilst eating
bread and olive oil

remembering their
final return

What comes next

curiosity kills where
piety leaves

but how to breathe
without knowing

what comes next

That's what you are

to the one speck of colour
bright smudge
noor
that's what you are
a brand new balloon
floating past grey windowpanes
that's what you are
the embers of my smile are
kept from dying
by your coos
your wide eyes
your forceful cry
you are capable of nothing
except propping up my
heart
like a tiny steel girder

The gift of existence

stop now on your
tiring journey
alight from your car
wrap your head
around this
you were not here
and now you are

Raptor

a peregrine
wrestles the whole sky
pelting down to curse
the quiet animal community
pulling like a black star
hands that rip
this bird is rolling with the power
now he's rolling with the thunder

one day
his eyes turned dark
with hunger

Vines

good grapes take time
these fruits are unmade wine
but why drink wine

when the grape can talk to you
just as well about the land
the time and the season

plus the grape is still sober
vines flexed and dark
left alone by soldiers

raised like children by the
motherly embrace of the sun
we were dust in the morning

and we'll be dust in the evening
when I left my land
there was no war

and there were no grapes
now the damage seems done
yet after long years

my uncle passes one to me
from my own farm
and it tastes just as sweet

as I thought it would
or even sweeter like
eating a beautiful word

the softest blush
it burns and soothes
all my tired hearts at once

Shere Khan

one night
beneath
the magnificent moon

I sat ensconced
in my dream
where came the cat

robed in power
each stripe a black
ceremonial dagger

Shere Khan was not
in the wrong
he was just the first

to be hunted
caught off guard
alone upon dark

and silky roads
where noble tigers
learn to trade in blood

that's it
I thought
this tiger needs a hug

This bond

it's late
the city
new
hair
hers
daughter
day
fades
blood
is thicker
this bond can
bend but
never snaps

Rain sounds

little brown animals
quaking in the rain
wax pushing off raindrops
earthy colours are bleeding
the pen the map the soil
sodden and rich
body heat is sliding
hearts will waver
that's when I know to climb
under branches
to build a leaf house
again England will become medieval
the screen will flicker
pulling darkness along old rails
my head is full
of wool and cashmere
then nothing but rain sounds
listen
the fizz the pad the hiss

Parenthood (middle)

home sweet home seed
grown up little tree
your feet should be firm now
soft wind
open sea

night night candlelight
pale-eyed clear sight
I'm hanging on your every word
just tell me
you're alright

Scouts

black Irish
sending dogs before them
oily coats slipping
through thistles
down the hills
and for the ambush
of the Romans
six banner holders
blades warm in the sun
easy in their
hearts and minds

No soul

are you one of those
people who sleepwalk
their way in and out
of my dreams

or are you one of those
who sit so deep you
don't even come up
to greet me in sleep

because some souls
feel so fundamental to us
but no soul is that fundamental
so shush now

and let me drift back to
that dream I had where
I drive a golf buggy
around New York

even though I've never
been to New York
and I don't play golf
I do drive though

Bagheera

and the world revolved
in his velvety ears

and gravity died
in the gloss of his fur

and he blunted his teeth
for the sake of his ward

and he gave him a home
in the soft and tranquil

settlement
of his dread black paws

Casino

no casinos here
not needed
enough wheels in
people's uncut lives
enough loss
empty wins
cheap velvet and
false grins inviting
in the great and good
to give up truth
for sex money
and more chips

Flyover

dissect down
to my heart
the flyover is rich
tonight the drive
is dark the warm
lights in stairwells
glimpsed in tower
blocks are stars
and my car is the moon

Your baby talk

I found it
in your tiny arms

around my neck you
lovely little boa constrictor

your baby talk
long cool rivers

of letterless riddles
not words as we know them

yet somehow
your eloquent giggles

make perfect
sense to me

The invitations

diagonally we pray
in houses where
no walls align
with what we believe

we're so far away
from Makkah now
bicycles parked near
lush potted

plants and snippets
of warmly lit bookshelf
from here
to the Holy City

one has to cross
a million thresholds
one has to forget
this townhouse

don't greet its stained
glass don't greet
the sleek black cat
who guards

its bright yellow door
tread on terracotta
tiles in bare feet
where no one

else can really see
you must climb
high out of reach
of busy streets

to access this land
you must step
over the chipped
hearth

you must turn
down the invitations
to anything other
than the unfurling

of your own path
it is open
vast
broad

straight
yours

Sakina (tranquility)
سكينة

come forward boy and tell us of a time
when your mind was clear and quiet

sands settled
horizon sharp as desert's jaw

no bleeding from this sky
only ultimate blue

inviting the bravest falcon
to mark its vast field

like the calligrapher's lost dot
and tell us of a time

in ancient hallowed rooms
sheltered now in England's hushed

castle grounds
bull rushes strewn over stone floors

fragrant
dark quilted walls

where sunset moats turn bloody
and the heron chats

on dusky flats
no

this *sakina* is not from us
it is given only to be savoured

and to wash minds
and to renew a wanderer's intention

Innocent orientalist

the untraveled traveller
tilts brows to the compass
and goes East for the very first time

Threadbare

like cousins greet cousins
my feet greet the ground
praying I lift my hands
to touch the world's edge

this is good like that white
light streaming through
eyelids asking you
to kiss the morning back

and it's good like a plum
whose cold flesh is so red
and juicy you'd better eat it
standing over the sink

and this is calming complete
like being tired out from
long walks in lively green
fells gently slapped

by knowing winds
hardy sheep lifting their
hooves over black rocks
hidden in grass

then we turn back
standing late in the kitchen
warm light and supple feet
once sodden and flat

now arched in the dry glow
from heel to toe soles
aching with happiness
this is good

for there are no more gaps
in the day anymore
the way my feet long to
stand upon well-worn mats

to pray like cousins
greet cousins
their open hearts love
as strong as it is threadbare

Parenthood (endings)

even doctors cry my girl
on rare occasions they have time
and the living all must
die my girl
their DNA unwinds
and from the moment we awake
we are designed to meet
with our appointed fate
but until then
you will always find me
here

Epilogue

all I know is written
after this line
flowing
and if you did not
study the whole measure
of your being
then it was beautifully wasted
and never run
from what's created
it is only the created after all

www.ingramcontent.com/pod-product-compliance
Lightning Source LLC
Chambersburg PA
CBHW021941040426
42448CB00008B/1173